a splash of co

Dennis Alexander

Romantic and Contemporary Piano Solos Designed to Enhance an Awareness of Imagery in Performance

Teachers are always searching for pieces which will immediately attract the attention of their junior high and high school students. My own students at this age always enjoy learning through the use of imagery, and I frequently resort to the use of various colors in hopes of stretching their imaginations to new heights. Some of your students may possibly think of other colors when playing these pieces, and of course that is not only good, but it is encouraged! The important point is that the music creates a response; the student should feel inspired by both the music and the power of imagination. I hope that the music will bring many smiles to your students' faces and give them a sense of renewed enthusiasm for practicing the piano. Enjoy!

Dennis Alexander

This series is dedicated with love and appreciation to my parents.

Alfred Music
P.O. Box 10003
Van Nuys, CA 91410-0003
alfred.com

Copyright © 1990 by Alfred Music
All rights reserved. Produced in USA.

ISBN-10: 0-7390-1316-5
ISBN-13: 978-0-7390-1316-8

Cover Photo
Paints and Brushes: © istockphoto / VikZa

forest green

blue boogie

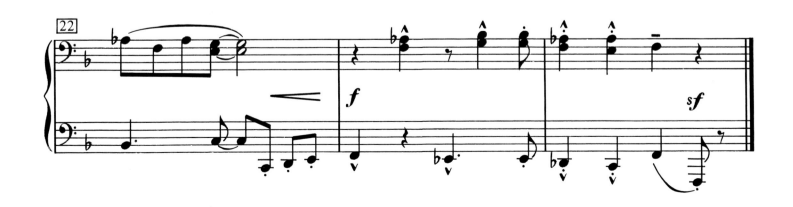

a touch of gold

for my friend Liz

pink tulips

gray granite

orange soda

Presto "fizzioso" (𝅗𝅥 = 116)

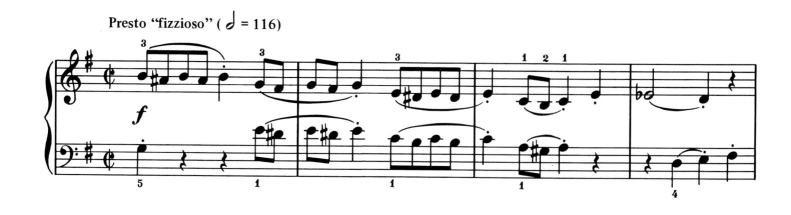

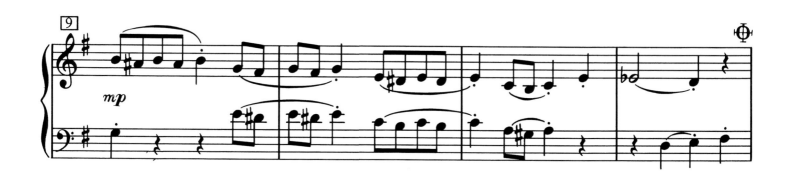

D.C. al ⊕, then Coda

⊕ *Coda*

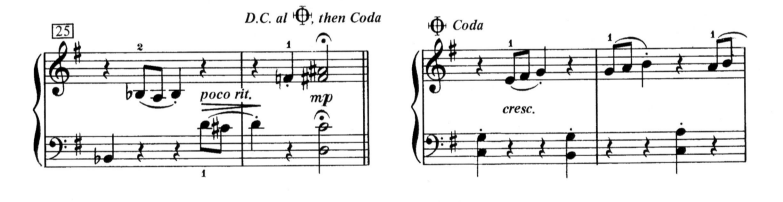